Screen Ti.

By

A. J. Donaldson

Illustrated

By

Penny Pearson

No part of this publication may be reproduced in whole or in part, or stored in a retrieval system, or transmitted in any form, by any means electronic, mechanical, printing, photocopying, recording, carrier pigeon, or otherwise, without the written permission from the publisher, except for the inclusion of brief quotations in a review. For information regarding permission contact the publisher.

Copyright © 2019 by Andrew J. Donaldson. All rights reserved.

Contents

Introduction………………………………… pg. 6

Section 1

Movement and Touch Exercises

Building a Mindfulness Den……….. pg. 17
The Bubble Dance………………………. pg. 19
The Big Squeeze………………………….. pg. 21
Simon Says Yoga…………………………. pg. 23
Musical Statues Yoga…………………… pg. 26
A Mindful Walk………………………….. pg. 28
The Twizzle……………………………….. pg. 30
Balancing the Books…………………… pg. 32
The Big Release………………………….. pg. 34
The Feather Stroke…………………….. pg. 36
The Tight Rope Labyrinth…………….. pg. 38

Section 2

Breathing Exercises

Sitali Breath……………………………… pg. 42
Lion's Breath……………………………… pg. 44
The Puffer Fish…………………………… pg. 46
Bunny Breaths…………………………… pg. 48
Cuddly Toy Breathing………………… pg. 50
The Big Bubble Stress Buster……… pg. 52

Section 3

Creative Mindful Exercises

Stress Balls……………………………… pg. 55
The Glitter Jar………………………….. pg. 57
The Scribble……………………………… pg. 59
Who's in control?……………………… pg. 61
The Gratitude Jar……………………… pg. 63
The Mindfulness Dice………………… pg. 65
Make Your Own Play-Doh…………. pg. 68

Play-Doh Meditation.......................... pg. 70
Play-Doh Mandala............................ pg. 72
Mandala Meditation......................... pg. 75
Write Yourself Happy........................ pg. 77
A Thank You Letter............................ pg. 80
Guided Meditation............................ pg. 83

30 Screen Time Solutions... An Introduction

A note for parents...

Let's be clear - being a parent is hard work. There's an endless list of things to think and worry about. And sometimes, even getting through the front door can feel a bit like hiking up Everest. (Who knew that packing a lunch, finding a toy, putting socks on stubborn feet, dealing with a toddler meltdown and negotiating a last-minute toilet stop was such hard work?) Then there are all the pressures of modern-day life...

Amongst all this chaos, the distraction of screen time can feel like a blessing. And I don't mean just for kids. After all, nearly all of us use handheld devices of some sort. As of 2019, roughly 70% of the world's population were using cell phones. That's 5 billion people burying their eyes into screens on a daily basis. Wow. Add on top of that all the laptops, tablets, consoles and televisions... Well, you probably get the picture.

Put simply, screens are unavoidable. They're everywhere. Almost compulsory. Which kind of begs the question....

WHAT ON EARTH CAN WE DO?

Well, if we can't avoid screen time, we have to learn to self-regulate it. This is true for both adults and kids, so picking up good habits while you're young, can set you on a life-long path to screen time solutions. So, without further ado, let's get started!

Regulating screen time...

First off, this book is not a crusade to ban all screen time. Nor is it a crusade against screen-wielding kids. (I'm not a big fan of crusades – they always seem to end in tears.) Used correctly, screen time has its benefits, and these need to be recognized. A few of them are listed below.

- Encourages communication with friends and family, particularly if they are far away.
- Provides educational input through interactive apps and games.
- Provides creative benefits through music, painting and drawing.

Even gaming (the twitchy parent's nemesis) has its own set of benefits. Don't believe me? How about improved brain speed? (Tick.) Enhanced memory? (Tick.) Improved coordination skills? (Tick, tick, tick...) All of which begs the following question... If screen time can be so positive, how on earth can we know when to stop....?

When to stop...

Let me help you out a bit. The real trick here is in recognizing negative symptoms; the behavior kids display when their bodies and minds have just had enough. (More of which, a bit later.) In time, kids can learn to monitor their own behavior and take screen time breaks at appropriate times. The mindfulness exercises in this book will help them to achieve this. But until then...

Guidelines for Screen Time by Age

Hallelujah for guidelines! Don't you just love them? They make everything black, white and easy. Well, sort of... The truth is, appropriate levels of screen time vary from child to child. That said, until you've got a handle on your own kid's behavior, it's handy to have a ballpark figure. The following guidelines may help.

0 to 18 months

How much screen time should babies have? Drum roll please.... Zero hours. That's right, babies shouldn't watch Sopranos boxsets on loop. Who knew? And the reasons for this are quite simple. Babies are fragile little things who need one-on-one attention: lots of eye contact, lots of play and lots of love. If there is screen time in their life, then it's best to keep it minimal - and avoid it being part of their routine.

2 to 5-year-olds

Are you ready for a bit of a shock? The recommended screen time for 2 to 5-year-olds is.... a single hour each day. That's right, responsible adults everywhere, just 60 measly minutes.

What's more, kids this age can't always decipher fact from fiction, so it's important to monitor their screen time content. Many TV shows are simply too overwhelming. This is particularly true of commercials.

So, what can you do? Stick to age-appropriate shows, preferably on a public channel, and you should be alright. That way, you'll avoid all the nasty commercials (as well as the inevitable nagging for toys that follows them!).

And finally, age 6 and above…

I call this the age of confusion. Why? Above the age of 6, there's no general consensus on screen time limits. That's right, no neat, recommended hourly guideline for a worried parent to cling to. Cripes.

The good news is this - if your child is engaged in a variety of activities (creative, mental and physical), then everything is probably fine. If you're still worried, check for the symptoms listed below. These will act as a warning flag for excessive screen time - letting you know when it might be time for a break.

The symptoms of too much screen time

- Lack of engagement in the real environment.
- Weak communication and social skills.
- Attention problems.
- Hyperactivity.
- Sleep deprivation.

If these symptoms are evident, the exercises in this book may help. Mindfulness has many, well-documented benefits – perfect for resetting a screen-frazzled brain. Try setting a timer for regular 'calm-time' top-ups. I'm sure that you'll notice a difference.

What is mindfulness?

Mindfulness can be defined very simply: it's about paying attention to the here and now. This encompasses a variety of things: your thoughts, your feelings, even the sensations in your body. Yes, mindfulness can be about contemplation; sitting quietly and still. It can also be about running around, jumping in the air and dancing.

What are the benefits?

Many! Mindfulness can have a positive impact on kids of all ages. In particular, it can help to:

- Reduce stress.
- Manage anxiety.
- Improve sleep and relaxation.
- Improve engagement with the real world.

Pretty cool stuff, huh? Now compare these positive outcomes to the negative symptoms of screen time, which we touched on earlier. Notice anything interesting? That's right - mindfulness is screen time's kryptonite! So, without further ado, it's time to get started!

Movement and Touch Exercises

Too much screen time (particularly gaming) can lead to a build-up of stress. This is caused by the release of hormones which need to be processed and find a positive outlet. Luckily, this is where movement can help.

It's time to get moving…

Movement, exercise and touch are the fastest ways to process hormone build-ups. When we get our children focused on physical sensations, we can help them to reduce their stress levels. That's less anxiety, fewer tantrums and less inattention. So, let's get active now!

Exercise 1

Building a Mindfulness Den

Children love making dens. Building a Mindfulness Den helps channel this creativity in a positive direction.

Age Range: Any. Younger children (5 and under) may need some help with construction!

Number of Participants: 1 or more.

You Need: Items to build your den with. (Pillows, blankets etc.)

The Aim: To create a quiet, comfortable space, perfect for integrating mindfulness into everyday life.

Technique:

1. Explore your home, gathering building materials. (Cushions, chairs, sheets etc.) Pay close attention to the items you're choosing. What do they feel like?
2. Build your den. Make it as comfortable as possible.
3. Try using the den for a breathing or meditation exercise. (You'll find some later in the book.) Why not invite a friend or a favorite toy?

Ways to Improve Your Den: Play soft music or add a few drops of lavender oil.

Exercise 2

The Bubble Dance

Parents, it's time to bust out your disco moves. Kids, don't worry, you can floss or dab instead.

Age Range: Suitable for all ages.

Number of Participants: 2 or more.

You Need: Music, bubble mixture.

The Aim: To focus on physical sensations and to burn up some energy.

Technique:

1. Play your favorite dance tunes.
2. Designate a bubble blower. Everyone else will be the poppers.

3. Start blowing! When the bubbles are floating, the blower calls out a body part. The poppers use this body part to pop the bubbles!
4. After 3 different body parts, swap the blower with a popper.
5. Repeat until you're all out of puff!

Top Tip: When the exercise is over check in on your body. What do you notice about your breathing? How about your heart rate? Try sitting still with your eyes shut until your breathing is normal.

Exercise 3

The Big Squeeze

We all need a hug sometimes. Learning to express self-love is a fantastic, stress-busting exercise - perfect for all situations and ages.

Number of Participants: 1 or more.

Age Range: Any.

The Aim: To provide a simple, sensory solution to stress. The Big Squeeze is easy to learn - and perfect for self-regulation. When you've been zapped by an alien in your favorite game, don't throw down your tablet…. give yourself a hug instead!

Technique:

1. Close your eyes and take 5 deep breaths. Try breathing in through your nose and out through your mouth.
2. Place your hands on to opposite shoulders. Your arms should be crossing your body.
3. Still breathing deeply, give yourself a squeeze.
4. Repeat until you feel calm.

Top Tip: Take this exercise into your everyday life. When a child has a meltdown, this is a great way to help calm them down.

Exercise 4

Simon Says Yoga

Yoga is the ultimate 'body' mindfulness. A brilliant exercise for enhancing flexibility, strength and coordination.

Age Range: 5 upwards.

Number of Participants: 2 or more.

You Need: The simple yoga poses in the diagram. (See next page.)

The Aim: To calm the effects of over-stimulation - allowing kids to center and come back to earth.

Technique:

1. Before you start, familiarize yourselves with the poses. When you can switch from one to another without falling over, you're probably ready to start!
2. Designate a Simon. This is the person who calls out the poses.
3. The participants listen carefully to the poses being called. If the call starts with 'Simon,' e.g. "Simon says, use the tree pose," the participants should obey. Calls without the word Simon should be ignored.
4. When a participant makes a mistake, they have to swap places with Simon.

Top Tip: Try inventing your own yoga pose. How long can you balance in it for? What will you call it and why?

Yoga Positions

The Tree   The Bridge

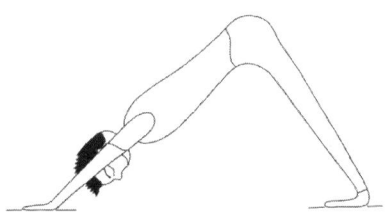

Down Dog

Cobra

Exercise 5

Musical Statues Yoga

Now you've learnt your yoga poses, why not use them in a different game? This will test your balance to the absolute max.

Number of Participants: 2 or more.

Age Range: 5 upwards.

You Need: Familiarity with basic yoga poses. (See exercise 3.) Calm, relaxing music.

The Aim: To focus on your body, the perfect antidote to over-active brains.

Technique:

1. Choose your caller. It is their job to start the music.
2. The caller calls out different yoga poses. Allow time for participants to move slowly between positions.
3. When the caller stops the music, participants must hold their positions. If they wobble or fall over they are out of the game!
4. When all participants are out, or if you want a change, choose a new caller and start again!

Top Tip: Try closing your eyes when you play. This helps you focus on your body and hold the poses for longer.

Exercise 6

A Mindful Walk

Fresh air, gentle exercise and mindfulness. Mix them together and what have you got? De-stressed kids and parents!

Number of Participants: 1 upwards. In a safe space (like an enclosed garden) children can carry out this exercise alone. That said, exploring's much more fun, in which case an adult should supervise.

Age Range: 3 upwards.

The Aim: To view the world through fresh eyes. Putting our focus on things around us: trees, flowers, even the hum of traffic noise, can help calm a busy brain.

Technique:

1. As you are walking, use your senses. What can you see, smell and touch? What sounds can you hear?
2. Can you describe things without using their names? This helps you focus on their qualities.

Top Tip: Using these techniques, play a multi-sensory guessing game. Describe what you can see, hear or touch. Can anyone guess what you're thinking of?

Exercise 7

The Twizzle

This exercise is a bit like a mental tongue-twister. By firing up both sides of the brain, it centers us emotionally and brings about a feeling of calm.

Participants: 1 or more.

Age Range: 5 upwards.

The Aim: This exercise is designed to help with stress, anxiety and sensory overload.

Technique:

1. Put your arms straight out in front of you, palms facing out.
2. Put one hand over the other at the wrists and weave your fingers together.

3. Turn your hands and arms inwards, towards your body, then place your clasped hands on your chest.
4. Cross your feet at the ankles and put your tongue on the roof of your mouth.
5. Stay still for a few minutes, breathing deeply. Done!

Exercise 8

Balancing the Books

Years ago, parents used this exercise to improve their children's posture. I think it works better calming down their minds!

Participants: 1 or more.

Age Range: 3 upwards.

You Need: A book. (Nothing too heavy.)

The Aim: To focus on a physical, balancing task.

Technique:

1. Pick up the book and balance it on your head.

2. Close your eyes and breathe deeply, focusing on staying balanced. Feel the weight of the book pushing down.
3. Set a timer, or count out loud. How long can you balance for?

Top Tip: It's easy to make this game more difficult. Try balancing on a single leg, or walking across the room. If you need to make it easier, try standing against a wall.

Exercise 9

The Big Release

A brilliant exercise for children and parents alike. The perfect precursor to sleep.

Participants: 1 or more. (With a parent to guide.)

Age Range: 3 upwards.

The Aim: To prepare for a good night's sleep. Try incorporating this exercise into your bedtime routine.

Technique:

The first few times you carry out this exercise, join in with your child to guide them.

1. Lie down in bed and shut your eyes.

2. Take 3 deep breaths, in through your nose and out through your mouth.
3. Tighten and release your muscles. Start with your toes. Curl them... relax them. Next stretch out your legs... relax them. Clench your fists... relax them. Stretch out your arms... relax them. Work up your body to your face. Now tighten your lips... relax them. Scrunch up your nose... relax it. Screw up your eyes... relax them.
4. Run a mental body check, noticing how you feel.

Exercise 10

The Feather Stroke

Warning: This could result in a tickle fight!

Participants: 2 or more.

Age Range: Any.

You Need: A feather.

The Aim: This is a simple exercise for switching focus. When a child's head is busy from screen time, ask them to concentrate on their body instead. Using the feather stroke is perfect.

Technique:

1. Stand opposite a partner. One person holds the feather, the other shuts their eyes. Roll any long sleeves up to expose your arms.
2. The feather holder strokes their partner. This could be on their face, arms or other bare skin. Stroke softly, slowly and gently, barely touching the skin.
3. After a couple of minutes, swap the feather and start again.

Top Tip: No feather? Try blowing through a straw, or stroking with a single finger instead.

Exercise 11

❈

The Tight Rope Labyrinth

Labyrinths follow a meandering course, gently winding from the outside to the center. Following their patterns helps generate calmness. Perfect for a screen time break!

Participants: 1 or more.

Age Range: Walking age upwards.

You Need: A piece of chalk or colored tape. If you're limited for space, try making a finger labyrinth with a paper and pen.

The Aim: To focus on the winding path and achieve a sense of calm.

Technique:

1. Use your tape or chalk to mark a line on the floor - anything from spirals to simple curves, snaking lines and zig-zags.
2. Walk the line tightrope-style, focusing on your balance and the labyrinth's pattern. Can you make it to the end?

Top Tip: If you're limited for space, make a finger labyrinth instead. Draw your labyrinth design on paper, take a deep breath, then trace the line with your finger. When you get to the center, follow the line back out again.

Top Top Tip: Try using your non-dominant hand. This makes it more difficult and helps you to focus.

A Finger Labyrinth

Breathing Exercises

✿

The next set of exercises are all about breathing. Apart from being portable and keeping us alive, breathing is also great for improving focus and calming us down. This is particularly true of kids. Using these exercises can help them to:

- A. Notice how they're feeling.
- B. Take a step back from overwhelming emotions.

Are you ready for a few less screen time tantrums? Me too. Let's get started straight away.

Exercise 12

Sitali Breath

Sitali is a Sanskrit word meaning 'cooling' or 'soothing.' When emotions are starting to fray, this exercise is brilliant for calming things down.

Participants: 1 or more.

Age Range: 4 upwards.

The Aim: To calm the effects of screen time stress.

Technique:

1. Stick out your tongue.
2. Roll up the sides to make a straw shape. (Note: it is genetically impossible for some people to do this. If you can't, then purse your lips instead.)

3. Shut your eyes. Imagine you're drinking a cold glass of water on a hot summer's day, sipping cool air into your mouth.
4. When your lungs are full, shut your mouth and hold your breath for a couple of seconds.
5. Breathe out through your nose.
6. Repeat 10 times.

Exercise 13

❀

Lion's Breath

Different types of screen time have different effects. The interactive, fast-paced nature of gaming can leave children hyper. Television, on the other hand, often de-energizes. When you've got things to do and places to go, 'Lion's Breath' can help get things moving.

Participants: 1 or more.

Age Range: 4 upwards.

The Aim: To transition from screen time to physical activity.

Technique:

1. Place your hands on your knees.

2. Take a deep breath through your nose.
3. Breathe out through your mouth with your tongue hanging out.
4. Say 'RA!'... LOUDLY!
5. Repeat 5 times.

Top Tip: The louder you say 'RA!' the better you will feel.

Exercise 14

The Puffer Fish

The humble puffer fish: true, it may not have the stature of the mighty lion. But for quick-fire stress-busting, it's my go to animal.

Participants: 1 or more.

Age Range: 4 upwards.

The Aim: An alternative to 'Sitali Breath', this exercise focuses on relaxing.

Technique:

1. Puff out your cheeks as far as they will go.
2. Hold the position for 5 seconds.
3. Release your breath.
4. Repeat 10 times.

Top Tip: Try this as an alternative. Take a deep breath in. Can you feel your tummy filling up with air? Imagine it's a balloon about to pop! Now take a series of small breaths out, each time losing a bit more puff. When you're fully deflated, start again.

Exercise 15

Bunny Breaths

What was that? You love stressed-out, hyperactive kids? Hop it!

Participants: 1 or more. (2 upwards for the active version.)

Age Range: 4 upwards.

The Aim: To achieve greater calm through focused breathing.

Technique:

1. Sit cross-legged on the floor. Take 3 quick breaths in through your nose, as if you're sniffing a carrot.

2. Hold the breath inside your body for a second. Release it back out, through your nose as slowly as possible.
3. Repeat 10 times.

Feeling energetic? Try the active version:

1. Designate a caller. The other participants are rabbits.
2. To start the game, the rabbits hop around the room exploring.
3. When the caller shouts stop, the rabbits sniff an imaginary item of the caller's choosing. (This could be a daffodil, a buttercup, some lettuce etc.)
4. Repeat until the rabbits have sniffed 10 items. To continue, swap the caller.

Exercise 16

Cuddly Toy Breathing

Kids love integrating their favorite cuddly toy into this exercise. Alternatively, they can rest a flat hand on their tummy.

Participants: 1 or more. (With a parent or guardian to guide.)

Age Range: Any

You Need: A soft toy.

The Aim: To pay attention to your breath and feel it in your body.

Technique:

1. Lie in a comfortable place with a cuddly toy on your belly.
2. Breathe in through your nose while counting to 3. Can you feel your tummy fill up? Check what's happening to the toy. Is it going up or down?
3. Breathe out again, to a slow count of 4. What is happening now? Which direction does the teddy go?
4. Shut your eyes and repeat 5 to 10 times.

Top Tip: Use this exercise if your kids have had screen time prior to bed. It will help them transition to a calmer headspace.

Exercise 17

The Big Bubble Stress Buster

Blowing bubbles is undeniably joyous and fun. It's also a great way to pay attention to your breathing.

You Need: Some bubble mixture and a blower.

Participants: 1 or more.

Age Range: Any

The Aim: To pay attention to your body, breathing and emotions.

Technique:

1. Picture in your head the bubble you're about to blow. You're aiming for the biggest, most brilliant bubble ever.
2. Take a slow, deep breath in through your nose. Focus on your body. You should feel your tummy blow up like a balloon.
3. Blow out gently through your mouth, making your bubble. Imagine it filling with all your bad thoughts and feelings.
4. When the bubble is ready, let it float away. Pop it with your finger. Keep blowing bubbles and releasing your negative emotions.

Top Tip: Repeating this exercise will increase its benefits. Pay close attention to your emotions. How do they change when you pop a bubble?

Creative Mindfulness Exercises

❦

All the creative activities that follow help ease kids into a mindful state. Like gaming, they encourage focus, concentration and absorption, but without the negative impact. (Who ever heard of too much crafting?)

What's more, they also encourage an emotional connection. Art allows kids to express their feelings, without any fear of failure or judgement. So, turn off your screens, roll-up your sleeves and let's start making some stuff!

Exercise 18

Stress Balls

Squeeze and relax. Perfect for popping in your handbag, rucksack (or even a pocket), you can take these with you anywhere.

You Need: Diaper bags, rice, balloons and scissors. (Adult supervision needed.)

Participants: 1 or more.

Age Range: 4 upwards.

The Aim: To create your own stress balls.

Technique:

1. Fill a diaper bag with rice. (The ball should fit snug in your hand.)

2. Twist the top of the bag and place on a flat surface. Tuck the loose ends underneath.
3. Snip off the thin end of a balloon. Pull the remaining balloon over your rice ball.

Using Your Stress Ball: Squeeze the ball as you breathe in through your nose. Release it as you breathe out through your mouth. Repeat 10 times, or until you feel calm.

Top Tip: To make your ball more attractive, use balloons of different colors. When the ball is complete, try snipping small holes in the outer balloon. This will reveal the color underneath. Funky!

Exercise 19

The Glitter Jar

There is something magical about these jars. Just like snow globes, you shake them up, then watch as the glitter settles. Brilliant for calming busy brains.

You Need: An empty jar and glitter glue (or glue and dry glitter).

Participants: 1 or more.

Age Range: 3 upwards.

The Aim: To actively demonstrate the benefits of mindfulness. Shaking the jar creates a storm (a bit like our heads when we're angry). By watching the glitter settle, we can see how bad feelings subside.

Technique:

1. Fill your jar almost to the top with water.
2. Mix in a single, heaped tablespoon of glitter glue (or your glue and glitter).
3. Replace the lid and shake!

Top Tip: Try using your glitter jar for regular screen time breaks. When your children are gaming or watching videos, set a countdown timer. When the alarm bell rings, ask your children to shake the jar. When the jar has settled again, allow them to continue.

Exercise 20

❀

The Scribble

Everyone can scribble! What's more, it's an excellent way to vent your pent-up frustrations.

You Need: A piece of paper and coloring pens or pencils.

Participants: 1 or more.

Age Range: Any.

The Aim: To externalize pent up anger. To promote creativity and lead towards meditation.

Technique:

1. Pick up a pencil. Imagine your stress flowing down your arm and making it move. Cover your paper with a scribble.
2. Now close your eyes. Take 3 deep breaths, in through your nose and out through your mouth.
3. Finally, color in your scribble, filling in all the spaces. Notice how you can turn your anger into something beautiful.

Top Tip: Comparing scribbles helps us understand our emotions. Try coloring in a good mood. How does your scribble look different?

Exercise 21

Who's in control?

Are you feeling stressed? Angry? Out of control? Take charge of your emotions with a mindfulness remote control.

You Need: A piece of paper, some card (a piece of cardboard box is perfect), scissors, coloring pencils.

Participants: 1 or more (with an adult to supervise).

Age Range: 4 upwards.

The Aim: To help recognize and regulate our emotions.

Technique:

1. Glue your paper to the cardboard.
2. Draw the shape of your controller and cut it out. (You can look at game controllers or television remotes for ideas.)
3. Color in your controller and add the buttons. Think about the buttons' actions. How will they help you calm down? 1 button might mean taking 10 deep breaths. Another, giving yourself a hug.
4. When you're feeling frustrated or grumpy, zap yourself!

Top Tip: Make your controller larger than life. This leaves room for writing on the buttons' actions.

Exercise 22

The Gratitude Jar

Finding things to be thankful for is a powerful way to shift a negative mindset. The more things you think of, the better you will feel.

You Need: An empty jar, paper, coloring pencils, assorted sweets, beads or other small items.

Participants: 1 or more. Due to small items, adult supervision is required.

Age Range: 4 upwards.

The Aim: To broaden emotional horizons beyond the screen. To experience optimism, enthusiasm, love, joy, and happiness!

Technique:

1. Fill an empty jar with colored sweets, buttons or beads.
2. On your paper draw colored circles. These should correspond to the colors in the jar.
3. Label your circles with 'gratitude' categories. For example, red could mean 'people,' yellow 'toys' and so on…
4. Eyes shut, pick out a bead or sweet from the jar. Check which category it matches. Who or what can you think of to give thanks for? Consider what makes them so special.

Exercise 23

The Mindfulness Dice

Fun to make and loaded with positive outcomes, The Mindfulness Dice will leave you in a better place.

You Need: A sheet of paper or card, a pencil/pen, glue, scissors.

Participants: 1 upwards (with an adult to supervise).

Age Range: 4 upwards.

The Aim: To provide a range of screen time breaks - perfect for calming children down.

Technique:

1. Copy the dice template on the next page onto a sheet of paper. (Alternatively, Google 'dice template' and print off the image!)
2. Choose 6 mindfulness exercises, writing one on each square.
3. Cut around the template and fold along the lines.
4. Glue the flaps and stick the sides together, forming a cube.
5. Leave to dry.

Top Tip: Why not make a yoga dice as well?

Dice Template

Exercise 24

Make Your Own Play-Doh

Squish, pound, pinch and mold your way to happiness. A super-fun way to bust that screen time stress.

You Need: 2 cups/260g flour, 1 cup/130g salt, 1 cup/235ml water. Optional - food coloring, essential oils.

Participants: 1 or more (with an adult to supervise).

Age Range: 4 upwards.

The Aim: To focus and find calm through physical sensations.

Technique:

1. Mix the flour, salt and water together to form a dough. Too dry? Add a few drops of water. Too wet? Add a little flour.
2. Optional - When the dough is formed, add a few drops of food coloring to brighten it up. Try essential oils, particularly lavender or chamomile, to improve the dough's calming effect.

Exercise 25

Play-Doh Meditation

Brilliant for recognizing urges. When there's Play-Doh in your hand, all you want to do is squeeze!

You Need: Play-Doh. (See the previous exercise.)

The Aim: To pay close attention to sights, sounds, smells and sensations.

Participants: 1 or more.

Age Range: 5 upwards.

Technique:

1. Play some calming music. Sit in a comfortable, relaxed position.

2. Hand each participant a small ball of Play-Doh. Before squishing, take a few deep breaths. Think about the feel of the Play-Doh. What does it make us want to do?
3. Start squishing the dough and consider its properties. Is it hard or soft? Warm or cold? What does it smell like? How does squishing it make you feel?
4. Close your eyes and concentrate on the feeling of the dough.
5. Finish the meditation with a few deep breaths.

Top Tip: For variation, ask the participants to mold specific shapes. Can they make a sphere? How about a sausage or a pancake?

Exercise 26

Play-Doh Mandala

Mandalas are circular patterns with repeating colors and shapes. They commonly occur in nature. Now you can add to nature's collection.

You Need: A ball of Play-Doh (see exercise 24), a piece of wax/baking paper, PVC glue, a selection of decorations (seeds, beans, shells, beads etc.).

The Aim: To create a mandala from Play-Doh.

Participants: 1 or more (with adult supervision for baking).

Age Range: 4 upwards.

Technique:

1. Roll out a ball of dough on the wax/baking paper to make a flat circle.
2. Decorate your mandala. Start at the center with a small circular design, then work your way outwards. Press your decorations into the dough to set them in place.
3. Air-dry for 3 to 4 days. Alternatively, bake in the oven at 200 degrees Celsius for about 10 minutes.
4. Allow the mandala to cool and dry. Coat it with PVC glue.

Top Tip: Collect your decorations on a nature walk. Small leaves, seed cases and petals are perfect.

A Play-Doh Mandala

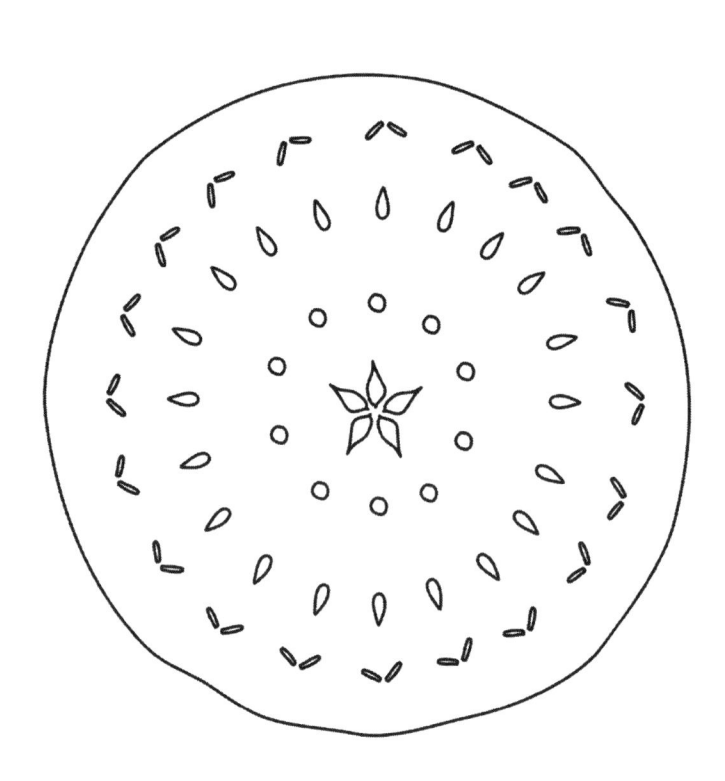

Exercise 27

Mandala Meditation

Meditating (even for a few minutes) is a brilliant way to reset screen-frazzled brains.

You Need: A mandala. You can use your Play-Doh Mandala from the previous exercise.

The Aim: To provide a counterpoint to the fast pace of gaming.

Participants: 1 or more (with an adult to guide).

Age Range: 5 upwards.

The Technique:

1. Find a comfy place to sit down. Take 3 deep belly breaths.

2. Examine your mandala. Focus on the center of the design, taking slow and steady breaths.
3. Now let your gaze wander. Notice the design, colors and lines on the mandala. Keep on breathing slowly.
4. For the last minute, close your eyes. Can you remember what the mandala looked like? Try recreating the patterns in your mind.
5. Open your eyes. Complete the meditation with 3 deep belly breaths. Done!

Top Tip: How long should you meditate for? A simple guideline is 1 minute per year of age. 6-years-old equals 6 minutes of meditation. Easy!

Exercise 28

Write Yourself Happy!

Writing's a great tool for reinforcing a positive image of yourself; setting in stone all the good things about you and your body. What's more, with a bit of encouragement, it can also be fun.

You Need: A pen and paper.

The Aim: To create a positive self-image through a series of positive affirmations.

Participants: 1 or more (with an adult to set up and help).

Age Range: 5 upwards. (If your children are too young or don't enjoy writing, check out the top tip!)

The Technique:

1. Copy the sentences onto a piece of paper. (1 set of sentences per child.)
2. Ask them to fill in the blanks. They can use the suggestions in the brackets or generate their own.
3. Complete the sentences. Encourage the children to think of all the things they're good at.

Sentences:

I _____ (child's name), am totally _____ (amazing/brilliant/fantastic).

I am even greater than _____ (favorite toy or game).

I am good at lots of things, but the thing I'm best at is _____ (sport/reading/drawing).

I am so _____ (grateful/happy) for my amazing life.

Top Tip: If your kids don't enjoy writing, let them dictate and write for them. If the exercise is too short, think up your own sentences and add them at the end.

Exercise 29

A Thank You Letter

Expressing gratitude can supercharge your happiness. Write a thank you letter today. I'm sure that you'll notice a difference.

You Need: A pen and paper.

The Aim: To explore the feeling of gratitude and how it makes us feel. To broaden our world beyond the limits of a screen.

Participants: 1 or more. (As with the previous exercise, an adult can write on the child's behalf.)

Age Range: 5 upwards.

The Technique:

1. Encourage the participants to think of helpful people. Start with obvious choices (family, friends etc.), then broaden the selection. How many people can you think of?
2. Choose a person to write a thank you letter to. What is so special about that person? Think of 3 things you want to thank them for.
3. Write your letter using the template. (Older children can expand on these ideas further.)

Top Tip: Expressing gratitude is the perfect way to end each day. Spend some time talking about the good things that have happened: the people who made you laugh, the people who helped you, and the things you did that were fun.

Letter Template

Dear_____,

You're such a special and amazing person. I just wanted to say a big thank you for_____. You make my life better by_____. This makes me feel_____ and I'll always be grateful.

Lots of love,

_____

Exercise 30

Guided Meditation

Breaking news... Children aren't always good at sitting still! When it comes to meditating, that can be a problem. Guided meditations can help, though. They improve engagement, which encourages a calm state of mind.

The Aim: To relieve stress and overthinking. To break unhelpful thought patterns.

Participants: 1 or more (with an adult to read the meditation).

Age Range: 5 upwards.

The Technique:

1. The participant needs to find somewhere comfortable to practice the meditation. He or she can meditate either sitting or lying down.
2. Ask the participant to take a nice deep, belly breath - in through the nose and out through the mouth. Repeat this several times.
3. Read the following script.

Journey to the Magic River

✦

As you breathe, you notice your body relaxing. You feel calm and safe. Your body feels loose. All your troubles are drifting away. Take one last deep breath, in through your nose and out through your mouth. Well done! You are ready for a magical adventure!

Imagine you are walking on a path through a field of tall, swaying grass. The sun is warm, the grass smells sweet, and butterflies flutter around you. As you turn a corner, the path enters a beautiful forest and the air is filled with birdsong. The leaves above glow like jewels, and a gentle breeze tickles your skin. The deeper you walk into the forest, the better you seem to feel.

Listen. The birdsong is getting quieter now. Gradually, the forest falls silent. Up ahead, you can hear a new sound: the rush and tumble of water. You break into a clearing filled with sunshine. In front of you, a majestic waterfall roars from the sky to land in a shimmering river. Rainbows fill the air. It's the most beautiful thing you've ever seen. You decide to stop for a rest.

Next to the river is a soft, springy patch of grass. You lie down, shut your eyes and rest your head on the ground. The sound of the rushing water relaxes you. Your troubles are all washed away. Any difficult thoughts, worries, problems... One by one you imagine them dropping in the water. In a flash, they are gone, carried away. Peace floods through your body. Your mind is free and clear. You continue to lie quietly and enjoy this magical feeling.

Now, listen carefully; this is important. You can visit here whenever you want. Wherever you are, just shut your eyes, take a deep breath and imagine you're back by the river. You will be here straight away. But for now, when you're ready, take a deep breath and open your eyes....

Top Tip: After meditating, check in on your feelings. How do you feel different?

Exercise 31

The Book Review....

Did you really think I was done?

First of all, thank you for reading. I genuinely hope that the book has been useful.

Secondly, please consider asking your child to leave an Amazon review (even if it's just a smiley!). This will help me to reach more children with these awesome exercises.

Thanks again and all the best,

Andrew Donaldson

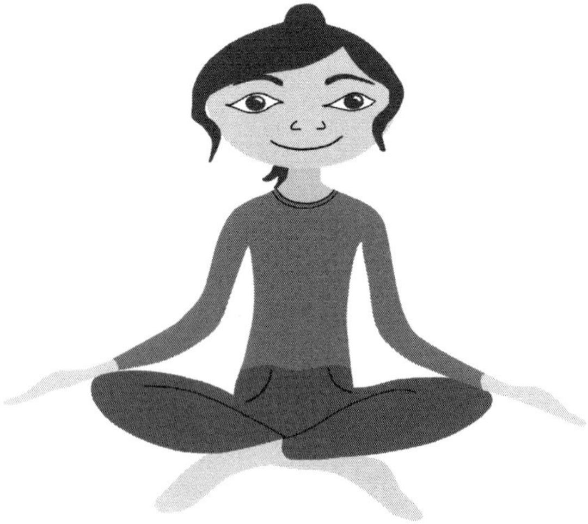

Printed in Great Britain
by Amazon